**LEAK**

# LEAK
## KATE HARGREAVES

BookThug · 2014

FIRST EDITION
copyright © 2014 Kate Hargreaves
cover image: "Musculi Colli" by Nadine Leduc

A **bundled** eBook edition is available
with the purchase of this print book.

CLEARLY PRINT YOUR NAME ABOVE IN UPPER CASE
**Instructions to claim your eBook edition:**
1. Download the BitLit app for Android or iOS
2. Write your name in **UPPER CASE** above
3. Use the BitLit app to submit a photo
4. Download your eBook to any device

The production of this book was made possible
through the generous assistance of the Canada
Council for the Arts and the Ontario Arts Council.

**Canada Council
for the Arts**

**Conseil des Arts
du Canada**

**ONTARIO ARTS COUNCIL
CONSEIL DES ARTS DE L'ONTARIO**
an Ontario government agency
un organisme du gouvernement de l'Ontario

LIBRARY AND ARCHIVES CANADA
CATALOGUING IN PUBLICATION

Hargreaves, Kate, author
     Leak / Kate Hargreaves.
Poems.
Issued in print and electronic formats.
ISBN 978-1-77166-056-3 (PBK.).–ISBN 978-1-77166-068-6 (HTML)
     I. Title.
PS8615.A727L42 2014   C811'.6   C2014-904788-6
                       C2014-904789-4

PRINTED IN CANADA

*for Jessie Tetley*

# Contents

# Heap

## HEAP

She heaps.

She heaps dirty clothes and dishrags on the stairs.

She heaps her plate with Brussels sprouts.

She heaps her teaspoon with brown sugar, stirs it into oats.

She heaps the compost.

She composts heaps.

She mounds.

She piles.

She piles old newspapers on the bedroom floor.

She plies.

She plies with wool.

She pulls wool over thighs.

She pliés.

She pleas.

She only buys two-ply.

Her nose runs in her sleep.

She rubs the sleep from her eyes.

She thighs in her sleep.

Hives cover her thighs.

She smears calamine on her skin.

Washes ink from her hair.

She lather rinse repeats. She dries.

Piles towels in the tub.

Heaps dress and tights in the sink.
She scrapes her leg.
Scratches. Loses sleep.
Heaps blankets on the floor.
Hives warm.
Nails out.
She seeps.

→ about woman and
→ heaps of food on plate
→ heap (Not feeling so good)
→ youre a "heap" hint of not taking
care of your body / run down

## SPLINTER

*[handwritten: Running. Shin splints]*

Windsor splints me. Splints shins—feet bat-battering asphalt
cracks thud thud thwack thwack thwack thwack shoelace plastic
tip clipping concrete. *thfooooo*—exhale fast against damp armpit *[handwritten: → humity]*
air. Pause one foot on pavement, other shoe rolling over ants
and grass and woodchips two feet from dog shit sizzle in the
haze. *thhoooo*—exhale re-tie loop over around and through, tie
the ears together and tap toe towards sneaker end. Stand. Sweat
slips between vertebrae, over spine juts like waterfall rocks—slish
slide slim. On feet and level with horse heads over sparse hedge
over-pruned by ninety-five degree weeks and days, nights of dry
roots, brown branches, crisp. Rind warming in racer-back lines,
heat-dying Friday afternoon onto shoulders arms and calves.
Out and back: laterals around perambulator pushers and camera
couples pausing to snap the elephant and her babies. *thfoooooo*—
*thfooooooo*—hard breaths in time with *glitter on the wet streets*
calves and quads suck blood and $O_2$ from head spinning and
concrete clumps cling to clay soles. Windsor sticks to my
sneakers, sod, cement, gum, cast-iron eggs and birds catch on my
laces. *thfooooooo*—exhale, and scuff rubber on road, to scrape off
stones, cedar chips, Tim Horton's cups and spare change. Shin
splints. Cable-knit air chokes my out-breath. *thf*—bronze base *[handwritten: geo locator]*
casts over my shoes. Drags me toward river railings and drills
toes into sod. Headphones pumping *dance dance dance til your*

*[handwritten: → humity of the place]*

13

*dead* at path-side. Playlist over. Riverside runner: artist unknown.
Bronze, textile and sports tape. Splint into the soil.

## 100% ALL-NATURAL ORGANIC BLEND

Her belly swims. Her belly measures 28 inches in circumference.
29 after a big lunch or too much salt. Her belly voted for the N D P.
Her belly skirts. Her belly shorts the bartender sixty-five cents on
the tab for three Molson 67s. Her belly pops buttons. Her belly
re-buttons. Her belly out. Her belly lifts. Her belly pours bran
flakes into tiny mountains. Her belly refuses to come outside
and tan with the others. Her belly gargles. After which, her belly
smells minty fresh. Her belly plans for the future: peanut butter
and raspberry jam on whole wheat toast for dinner, an apple and
coffee tomorrow morning. Two coffees for lunch. Black. Her belly
pouts. Her belly demands discipline. Her belly lacks willpower.
Her belly laughs annoy the people two rows behind at *Pineapple
Express*. Her belly tender. Her belly bruise. Her belly picks up bad
language at school. Gosh. Her belly collects dust. Her belly fat to
hip fat ratio factors into calculating her risk for diabetes and heart
disease, alongside family history, geography, and literary studies.
Her belly barely stomachs bananas. When she jogs up the stairs
her belly wobbles. When she sings her belly takes minutes. When
she goes out for dinner her belly house-sits, feeds the dog, and
lets him out for a piss. Her belly barks. Her belly pants. Her belly
never squeezed into a size three. Her belly forgets to return text
messages. Her belly wakes him up at four in the morning. Her
belly swells in August. Her belly bloats in November. Her belly

inputs height, weight, age and sex to calculate an accurate body fat percentage.

Her belly re-calculates.

Her belly re-calculates.

Her belly believes in a small margin of error. 3.7 percent. Her belly re-calculates. Her belly believes in a somewhat substantial margin of error. Her belly floats. Her belly isn't half as hairy as his. Her belly glows in the dark. Her belly never has to compete with her hips. Her belly never learned to jump rope. Her belly walks. Her belly floats. She fills her belly with paper and ink. She chews her nails. She bites the insides of her cheeks. She licks her elbow crook sweat. She gnaws her shirt sleeves. Her belly of iron instead of abs of steel. Belly of iceberg lettuce and 0% M.F. plain yogurt. Her lose-belly-fat-fast. Her walk-off-five-pounds-of-belly-fat-before-Memorial-Day. Her hyperbole. Her belly glows in the park. Her belly doesn't "do" spaghetti. Herbally, she has other uses for oregano. Her belly munches. Her belly manages the organic grains department at the new FreshCo. Her belly manages. Her black dress sags at the hips. Her belly buys stocks in quinoa. Her belly byes.

## RIBFEST

Her ribs snap. Her ribs tickle. Her ribs protrude approximately
the same distance as her breasts when her push-up bra is in the
wash. Her underwire sticks her in the ribs. Her ribs bruise and
swell. Her ribs taste better sans barbecue sauce or Tabasco. Her
top right rib broke in a Slip'n Slide accident when she was nine
and healed on its own leaving a large deposit of bone jutting out
of her chest that makes wearing a bikini top in public lopsided.
Her collarbones. Her sternum. Her rack. Her ribbed for her
pleasure. Her vote for your favourite rib recipe from our forty-
two vendors this weekend only at. Her stick to your ribs. Her ribs
stick. Her ribs clatter against one another inside her chest. Her
ribs pierce her lungs every time she quickens to a jog. Her spare
tire. Her spare ribs. Her spare hips. Her spare vertebrae. Her ribs
spent all day Sunday in bed while she cleaned out the crawlspace.
Her ribs cage. Her ribs leak marinade all over the wool. Her ribs
collapse under the boning. Her. Rib. I. She prefers ribs with a
little less meat on the bone. Her ribs don't see eye to eye. Her eyes
rib and slit. Her ribs took off in the middle of the night. Her ribs
might come back if they smell the bowl of milk she left out on the
porch. Her knit one purl two rib one.

*Handwritten annotations: "Sweet / spicy", "sanctity", and a small mark.*

## TOENAILS

*after bpNichol*

1. I could bite you. As an infant foot-in-mouth and foot-and-mouth until my feet were feet away so far down my legs that I couldn't dream of bending them up to my face or even touching them fingers to toes straight-kneed. Toenails as markers of flex-prowess, glinting in yoga-mat leg lengths. Measure the gap between finger and toe nail. I cheated. Bent my knees and mat clattered finger and toe nails together. Matte.

2. As in in-grown nail, but aren't they all in-grown-out from the nail bed? A jag-edge shard my skin overgrew tender, warm, and red. Gotta dig it. Can you dig it? Scalpel toe clenching doctor a foot and corn and callus specialist scraping hot skin searching for nail scraps. Digging for bones or scraping weed roots. Tweezer plucking culprit cartilage. 40 dollars and 4 x 4 gauze.

3. High heels versus ballet flats you lost to the stiletto that stilleto-toe stomped you big toe. Lost the other to her dance partner's oxford step. Two crunches on the dance floor a yelp and a limp. Sidelined for the last two songs. Tights off pulled by the toes under covers in the groom's parents' basement. Good morning black nails. Purple black ombré paint and the next week you shattered in my sock. Black toe veneer souvenirs skin bare pink. I

painted you red and stubby lacquered the skin. Red flesh and top coat. Lifted necro nails to the toilet and flushed.

4. I dig you. Dig you with the nail scissors and a toilet paper wad. Brush the yellow crumbs out—you grew back sick and detached. Split from the skin. Soak you well in salts and mouthwash. Dye feet teal. Purple. Dip in tea tree. Smear Vaporub. Eucalyptus toes crumbling yellow and cool into sock seams.

5. He toenail sliced my heel. Rolled over in bed and kicked. Ankle meet jagged edge. *Frrrrrrrrip.* Collect blood and skin flakes under nail bed and bedsheets. I told you to cut those toenails. Mmmmmm hmmm. Rolls over again. Mmm hmmm I did.

6. Wanted to dance ballet. Soccer cleats instead of toe shoes. Better for your toesies. Dancers lose their toenails, crush their toes. Bruise black. Don't kick from the toe. Toe the line. Turn out your toes. Your nails didn't turn out. Didn't nail that shot. Another nail in the coffin. Spittin' tacks. Spitting nails.

7. Can't stop biting my fingernails. Can't reach my toes. Carry a nail file and never grind. A nail file on the bus. On a walk. On the move. Toenails are sharp. Files sharper.

## CHIROPRACTICE

Her back slides. Her back slings. Her back can't reach the
recycling bin under the sink. Her back responds well to electric
shock therapy. Her back tracks. Her back to the futures. Her back
makes an appointment with a licensed chiropractic professional
twice a week for the next sixty days. Her back burns, peels, burns
again. Her backless dress cuts too low for a bra. She backdates
her chequebook. She backs out of dates. Her back bones reflect
three times over in the mirrors at H&M. Her back sticks to the
vinyl booth at Burger King. Her ribs. Her spine. Her binding. Her
bound. Her back tingles when she raises her arms in the air. Her
back googles: back, numbness, WebMD, symptoms, serious. Her
back on a Sunday. Her back to front. Her back leaks self-tanner
through a white T-shirt. Her back dripping. Her backed into a
corner. Her back braces for the storm. Her back skipped rent day.
Her backpay barely covers the electrical. Her back to the wall.
Her back-to-back, chin-to-chin, face-to-face. Her on her back.
Back seat. Back and forth. Backwards day. She puts her back into
her work. She leaves a cloth on the back burner. She forgets to
turn off the stove. She gets her back up. She starts a backfire. Her
back re-burns and blisters. Her back sweats through her dress.
Her back rests. Her back strikes. Her back pickets. Her back
twinges when she picks up a sign. Her backbiting. Her nail biting.
Her ankle biting. Her back to the apartment after walking twelve

blocks, to make sure she locked up. Her back out into the rain.
Her back down. Her step on a crack.

→ Sports injury?
→ also back as in "strong backbone"
→ whats keeping her together
→ her back googles "back of mind.)
→ her back on a Sunday = laid
back
→ her back slipped rent / it slipped
the back of her mind.
→ her backed into a corner / she feels
trapped.
→ her step on a crack "breaks
your back"

→ Mental / physical deterioration.

## HIP TO BE SQUARE

Her hips sink ships. Her hips just don't swing. Her hips fit snugly in skinny jeans. Her calves won't squeeze in. Her hips check. Her hips cash in on the market for skin. Her hips max out their credit. Her hip-replacement value is greater than that for knees. Her hip socket pops out on the way up the stairs and back in on the way down. Her chiropractor takes the time to crack her hips. Her hips show through her slip. He slips. Hips shoot from the her. She shoots from the knee. Her hip-to-hip, toe-to-toe, or cheek-to-cheek. She toes the line. She hips the other cheek. Her hips print bruises on the wall. Walls purple her hips. Her hips yellow-belly. Her hips run. Her hips send a note threatening not to return unless working conditions improve. Her hips make the rules. Her hips call her gutless. Her guts call her hippy. Her hip flask calls in sick. Her rose hips. Her daisy dies on the windowsill. Her hips move home in steps. Her steps crack her hipbones. Her hipbones give whips. She de-bones thighs. Her thigh-highs slip. She's a sight for sore thighs. Her thighs join at the hip. Her hips end with thighs. Her ends are split. She splits her hips.

→ Size of someone who might be larger.
→ Someone allowing their size to define them
→

Chew

## CHEW

She chews three salteens at once.

She chews an orange peel.

She chews a stick of jerky.

She chews her bottom lip.

She chews the end of her sleeve and leaves a hole.

She chews the cap off her pen.

She chews the inside of her left cheek. She chews it up and spits it out.

She chews it over.

She chews him out. → *Angry*

She chews more than she can bite off. → *deals w a lot*

She chews her cud. → *deals w shit*

She chews tobacco. → *copes*

She chews the fat with the cashier at Tim Horton's while waiting for
her everything bagel with plain, light cream cheese and a blueberry
white tea with nothing in it because, she tells the cashier whose
nametag says Abe, their coffee really doesn't do much for her, sort
of like drinking bathwater, or the bottom of a rum and coke when
the ice has melted and you can really only taste water. → *many*
*say it*
*sucks but also*

She chews gum and walks at the same time. *explains her*

She chews nails. *state.*

She eschews.

She eschews her old friends.

She eschews a male escort.

She issues a parking ticket.

She issues takes. She takes issue.

She: "choose."

She achoo-s.

Sheet use.

Chez tu. ↳ at your place.

## PAPER LADDER

V.

*The final tier consists of processed food*
Vegetable ink makes guts grumble
Nose cracking the spine of a new book or film festival catalogue
ink licking cinnamon buns high fructose mayonnaise
six years at tier V with grilled cheese and bacon

IV.

*eating only from tier I and II will give you a near-perfect diet*
Throw out four full jars
nutella and jam fail the nutrition ladder
whole wheat toast climbs to the "happy tier"

III.

*you want to maximize the nutrients in every calorie you consume.*
Oil is tier V but I file ink at I,
newspaper at II.
Maybe III for thicker bond.
A list of tier I foods that give me heartburn:
cucumbers, avocados, honeydew melon
lick the ink off my fingers
leave blue smudges on the fridge
a lemon cake, one tier or three is still up at V

no listing for coffee cake means

two slices for breakfast

II.

*"raw, steamed, grilled, poached, baked, or broiled"*

Chew the inside of my lip all day and don't gain an ounce.

I would list gums no higher than tier II.

Skin mouth to stomach balances out.

Swallowing half a gram of loose lip

better than 40 calories of celery.

Cuticles, nails, thumb edges

add bananas for an

itchy neck

I.

*The first tier contains food choices that are the healthiest*

Tier I items I couldn't identify in a lineup:

amaranth, endive, collard, natto, spelt.

Amaranth: a language spoken in certain parts of Asia.

Collard and spelt both have something to do with mining.

Endive: a new enzyme in fifty-five-dollar face cream from behind
    the counter at Shopper's Drug Mart, and I could scoop natto
    into a plastic bag and seal with a twist-tie in the corner store
    candy aisle.

The cap of my pen: tier I

hard plastic
slip and cut my gums
have to up my iron intake
switch back to pencil for a lighter snack with more fibre.

## OFF-BALANCE

149 ¼: I should wash these curtains next weekend, at least before I pack and move; toothpaste smudges satin edges. 151: no halves or quarters, just even Steven. Steven weighs at least eight pounds less and he's likely three inches shorter. 151 ½: blueberry bran muffin, cream of sun-dried tomato soup, a whole wheat roll. 148: (minus the towel makes 147 ¼, subtract $^1/_{10}$ for the necklace and the 53 drops of water on my back, knots in my hair) equals 147 $^6/_{40}$, reduces to 147 $^3/_{20}$ reduces to. 149 ½: popcorn burst, olive oil, the corner of an eye: buy more cover stick, curl lashes. 150: to the bathroom to take it back down again. 151: three parallel red indents in rice pudding flesh: nylons, panties, skirt ══════════════ 146: Dan shaved off all the hair on his body, kept his lashes, stood naked in a gallery. 149: how many ounces make up an eyelash? How many lashes make up an ounce? 152: Toenail clippers, eyelashes, snip them at the lid. 149: At what point does all-bran becomes too much-bran? 149 ½: bruised my fingertip prying 3 AA batteries out of the V C R remote. 149.24: Mixtaper, typewriter, record player, not digital. 147.3: in the mail today: my mother's pattern for a crochet bikini c. 1973. 148.25: I round down to the nearest ¼. 148 ½ cup water. 150 ¾ tbsp maple syrup, a pinch of chili powder. 150 and half the time I spend pan-frying egg whites for dinner I could throw on a pot of coffee instead. 151: even at 10 A.M. 154: with a coat, jeans

and leggings. My ice skates still overlap at the ankles if I pull them taut enough. 150 ¼: six-hundred-and-one quarter pounders. 14.9 km from here through Walkerville around Sandwich and back. 154: *not legal for trade.* 151 words at ¼ ounce per word: edit. 150 dollars on new Tupperware. 152. 151.3 154.5. 14.8 bruises on thighs, hips, shoulders. 14 ¼ scarves to mail out in the morning. 149 stitches.

Doctors appointment

## LONG CENSUS

What is your waist to protein rah-rah ratio? Fill in box 32 with
your daily calamine intake. Where can I find your hipbones?
Be precise. How many days of the last 21 did you engage in
strenuous physical activity? (For a complete definition of
"strenuous," please see appendix four. Note that sexual activity
only records as strenuous in the circumstance that both partners
break a sweat. For a complete definition of "partners," see
appendix sweat). How many grams of complex carbohydrates—
how can you eat this shit it tastes like cardboard?—Chart your
height on the wall of your childhood kitchen and copy out into
the new apartment in pen. Graph your weight with this pie.
Three slices for a gain subtract the crust and start again in the
bathroom. Order egg whites at the Lumberjack. How many times
a month does 1% reduced sodium cottage cheese go on sale at
Shopper's Drug Mart? Bike six miles to the clinic for knee x-rays.
Wrap unwrap re-tense pre-tensor. Forget your nutrition guide
in a downtown Toronto condo. How many days do you have to
return that bikini for store credit? Can't you reach your toes? Big
girls can bend but I guess you get credit for licking your own
nose. After the warm-up before the stretch check your heart rate
with your official team monitor your consumption of peanut
butter banana—can't make it through the gritty mess to the
squirrels—where—where water—At what point do you pause to
pee? You should only discontinue use if you feel dizzy. Or sore.

## RESEARCH ETHICS BOARD

Went 28 hours on black coffee alone.
No paper record but
—you can write this down
dropped to
117.26.
Noise-cancelled the grumbles.
Packed an apricot a day and scraped
93 in Home Ec.
—need a transcript?
Planked over calculus and crunched
75, 76, 77
sanding down vertebrae on hardwood.
Passed out on the high jump mat before 800 m
tryouts (you're just *built* for the distance)
licked the chocolate off a Crunchie wrapper squatting west
stairwell on spare
faked cramps in the showers and
swapped latex for wool in September chem lab
sprouted goose down up my back
stockpiled tampons
stretched out in Dewey psych section 616
fell asleep in the stacks.

# ARC

**1.**

Arc under her skirts after lunch

shouldn't have bread cheese soup

in the office bathroom mirror untucks her blouse, zips down the
    skirtside zip halfway

checks for stall feet, checks the door and sneaks up on the arc
    peach and

two red lines indent from

the belt of her beige skirt

shouldn't have/eaten breakfast milk oats bran sip of grapefruit

breathes into ribs/breasts/shoulders and pulls the arc closer to her
    back

belly button pulls back, stretches tall from round to slit

Elle stands sideways hips jut in front, tummy arc bread and butter
    tied back with one breath

holding blouse bra-high with one hand, skirt up with the other

strain tight on her mouth, coughs

won't eat dinner.


**2.**

Elle unties the cord on her robe

yesterday she finished reading a novel that called it a housecoat

robe, yes, but something about housecoat

34

less regal, explains the bite marks and loose threads from where
    she gnawed the corner ends of the cords


3.

Elle unties her housecoat, slips her arms out and feels the rush of
    cold air across her belly
leaves the coat dangling from the hood, slipping down off the
    back of her head
sliding down over snips of hair that stick up in the back. Elle
    needs a shower.
stands naked in front of the full-length mirror with its pine edges
waist nipping in slightly under the ribs
small arc, belly button round
presses heels of both hands down under rib lines and slides them
    over the round bit
forcing the flesh inner and tauter and downer
a rumble inside a slosh lets go and again the arc
sideways won't concave in down through
profile: firm shoulder, small slope of breast hip hip and in the
    middle the blocking arc
Elle presses again squeezing air up or down just out out
but the arc rounds

4.

Elle

naked

like the past tense

was naked not is

Elle was naked

Who naked Elle?

Elle nakes

Elles nake

Elle naking


5.

damp in the bedroom Elle slips the warm towel off her head

black hair fuzzy and knotty

pulls up brown silk pajama bottoms legs sticking in small dark
    patches

shirtless in the mirror clasps both hands over tummy button

scowls and presses

the arc rumbles

sloshes with coffee

Elle picks up her houserobe wraps up sharp chest bones and soft
    tummy

wet hair under a terrycloth hood

Skim

## SKIM

She skims.

She skims the floating fat off his mother's minestrone soup.

She saves it in a Ziploc bag in the freezer.

She skims flat rocks across the sodden backyard.

They skip once and sink into the mud.

She skims the grass seed out of the water with a pool net.

She skims her milk. Sometimes she one percents.

She skims a little bit off the top at the office.

She scams.

She scans the ceiling for hidden cameras.

She skins her elbow on the brick wall.

She picks off the scab and tucks it into her purse.

She purses her lips.

She paints them pink.

She sinks. She misses.

She sinks her face into her towel.

She collects stray hairs from the bathroom sink.

She scrimps by the skin of her teeth.

She teethes.

She sinks her teeth into a stale bread roll.

She stinks of garlic and sweat.

She stings.

She scrapes the stinger from her foot.

She limps over to the sink.

She steeps a pot of tea.

She scans the bottom shelf of the fridge:

out of skim.

## HYPO

Take a left turn out of Chinatown to pick up an ounce of panic.
Six steps onto Hastings a slight pinch in the baby toe. Because
streets lined with junkies equals a two-to-one chance of sidewalk
syringes. Google needles and shoes back home, check your toe
check again check again, could that be a puncture no just a blister
from 18 km on foot but there would still be a sharp in your shoe
or the plunger underfoot so it couldn't have. Google results only
deal with city workers stuck in steeltoes under manhole covers
and shifting needle exchanges. Think you're well travelled read
*Trainspotting* at age 13 but couldn't sit through the film gave
blood eleven times and never passed out but never looked at
the needle either walk a city block past the woman shooting up
into her stomach and the guy selling in front of the community
centre. Sure you've been stuck. Dozens of women go missing this
end of town but you're going to bite your lip over a nine-dollar
beer in Gastown over the maybe syringe you didn't feel but may
have stuck you in the shoe walking home now running head-on
into strangers with maps scanning the pavement for anything.
Anything resembling. The slight pinch in the side of your baby
toe. Slight pinch. Take a left turn.

## HOME REMEDY

Forget the fourteen voicemails you declined to return.
I've been mixing up chlorine gas when I should be bleaching the
    toilet bowl,
soaking my toes in an empty margarine container with equal
    parts water and mouthwash, tingeing skin dental blue from the
    bottom up and padding minty fresh across the kitchen floor.
    *Special K* clings to damp calluses.
Message number seven re: the likely clot in my left calf
press into muscle with your thumbs. See, swelling groans and I
    can't seem to pull up my skinny jeans.
Message number eleven: voice wobble from the stand-on-one-
    toe-and-hop vein shake-up.
Breathing short croaks to pulmonary embolism or maybe the
    DIY poison gas
but my lashes started twitching so I'm calling poison control
to tell the operator my name's Kay and I'm 19, maybe 14, maybe
    Dee
no there's not a window in the bathroom but I can close the door
the line's cutting out—Message fourteen: dropped the phone in
    the toilet
anything to send some sparks down your line.

## HOW TO LOCK A JAW

1. chew gum.
2. gnaw fingernails to stub tips. raw pink and panging. popcorn salt hangnails.
3. bite pen end. paint mouth roof in ink eruption. blue tongue. tastes blue: blue freezie blue powder punch blue ink tastes like flax.
4. doorbell your neighbour. loaner pen. clutch an egg and one cup of sugar for trade. no answer. rest egg against *if you lived here you'd be home* mat. pour sugar in window box. water geraniums. door knocker sticky note. blank.
5. check in. bible notepad phone book remote control desk drawer. check out. no pen. too many stains in the bathtub. microwave-free. bedbugs. white towels not blue. twin not queen. left the door at home unlocked. credit card at the grocery store.
6. front desk room refund from 7b.
7. yawn.
8. molar pen cap tail flat. pick popcorn shards from teeth. spit.
9. gums. chew.

## SHOE-IN

One standard kitchen freezer fits 23 pairs of shoes
250,000 sweat glands per foot
left/right inside separate sandwich-size Ziploc bags
ballet flat / sneaker / pump / felt boot
rubbing up in the chill
slide nylon past leatherette
loose green beans, ginger root
through foggy plastic barriers
shrimp ring slumps
leaks pink through the floral tablecloth
ice packs warm by the windowsill
eight sandals slide lengthwise into the door
sweaty thawed pizza cardboard
drips a Hungryman dinner
meatloaf running into peach pie
2,887 units of bacteria per shoe
13 spring rolls, a pound of grey, lean ground beef
and a bag of Brussels sprouts
slip on the floormelt
limp room-temp pea bag surrounds an ankle bruise
green marbles drop out through a slit
roll over foot / soften between toes

## GARLIC

garlic you say, on the couch a bulb of garlic shedding papery
skin in the seams of our corduroy. I lint-brushed yesterday. how
will you explain away this one? a still-life sketch or too much
time watching re-runs of *Buffy*? home sick clocked out but garlic
never really kills the way stakes and holy water will. I ate four
cloves raw, they burned my lips and tongue but I chewed all
four chews and coughed, the pieces rubbing the way down my
swollen throat. garlic will keep the doctors away I told her once
in her office blood work requisition in hand garlic instead of
aspirins sucked from raw cloves not Buckley's syrup. eight once
before bed she said I hope your boyfriend's not a vampire. what
is that cheek pressing my burning neck your medicine smells like
my mother's house we eat pickled onions together out of the jar
English pickled onions in malt vinegar an onion the doctor says
keeps. cut your finger yellow scab boil an onion and wear it warm
like a poesy ring.

## APPENDIX 3

Straight arm jacks give me this pull in my hands like I'm
wearing stacks of pewter bangles on both wrists. When I opened
the barbecue last night my fingers tingled for a few minutes
afterwards which means that I am having a stroke phoning
Telehealth dialing with prickling digits and describing how my
tongue isn't numb thanks unsure that I am not stroking now
I've got this stabby feeling in my left side and I can't recall if the
appendix pangs in the left or right side before exploding and
going septic into guts but I can remember only to worry on the
opposite side from where the anatomy book shows the appendix
in the body, which doesn't help as I've just developed an itch on
the back of my calf and while the bump looks like a mosquito
bite I hear flesh-eating bacteria can look bitten on day one before
eating right through to your tendons and you need a sheet
between your face and leg in the hospital so you don't pass out
from the sight of your muscle inside-out in front of you. I wonder
if they use maggots to clean off the dead flesh when someone's
leg starts spoiling and the sheet really covers so you don't have
to watch maggots consume part of your inside-out appendage.
The tingling in my fingers when I dial 911 and a bit of pain in my
temple just on my right side but I can still remember long words
like onomatopoeia and stand on one leg until my itchy calf means
I have to switch legs but at least the ache in my stomach seems

to have become more of a churning as if I have eaten a rotten
slice of tomato or the sandwich artist, as Subway calls them, did
not wash her hands in correct correspondence with the posted
instructions and her germs have now made their way into my
gut, which I recall had a jabbing pain on the right or maybe
the left side meaning my appendix has exploded and my septic
body perhaps will kill off the flesh eating bacteria in my leg, the
tingling in my palms every time I barbecue, dial the phone, order
Subway, stand on one foot and practice straight arm jacks and
the onomatopoeia in my head that means I must not be having a
terminal stroke.

## ANTS

The ants are on their way.

They've surveyed the best route to the kitchen, through the hole behind the bathroom radiator, along the floorboards in the living room, under the closet door past the bread maker and TV set aside for next week's yard sale, around the corner past the cleaning cupboard, over the mop handle, onto the linoleum.

Behind the garbage they gather

crumbs of puffed wheat and the peel-off tag from a can of juice, sticky with orange concentrate.

They send scouts to scan for rolled-up newspapers and heels of palms.

They look up your skirt.

They crawl between your toes.

They know they can outrun you 75 percent of the time.

They prepare to take those odds.

The ants collaborate in your cereal box in the space between the plastic bag and the cardboard, surviving on stray cornflakes that fall between and start to go soft.

They take hits of Raid to boost their immune systems.

The ants collect pieces of your dead skin.

They imitate stray hairs brushing your calves. Hiding in the nook behind your knee.

Buying shares in all-natural cleaning products and promoting
them with 30-percent-off coupons at the local Sobey's on
Sunday.

Rubbing Raid-slathered bodies on the inside of the peanut butter
jar just enough to give you food poisoning.

They are licking peanut butter off each others' backs.

They drip Raid into your instant coffee.

The ants grow, first a quarter, then half, then an inch long. Soon
they will sit at your kitchen table ordering quiche lorraine for
dinner.

Soon you will be dinner.

The ants are coming to your kitchen.

You wipe down every surface with anti-bacterial cloths and a
50/50 mixture of
Borax and water.

You kill the scouts upon sight with the heel of your palm and
watch them twitch their legs after you crush their solid
middles.

The ants come marching two by two hurrah hurrah.

Eating your peanut butter and cornflakes.

Soon you will be dinner.

Pore

## PORE

She pores.

She pores over her psychology textbook.

She pores over the late-night pita menu.

She pours water over tea steeps and pours.

She pore-reduces. She scours.

She scrubs.

She pores over her blackheads in the mirror.

She skins.

She skins her ankle with a dollar-store pink plastic razor.

She nicks.

She grazes.

She snacks at half-hour intervals throughout the day: trail mix,
   dried cranberries, arugula, celery.

She scans the fridge for leftover spinach.

She pours olive oil and vinegar on lima bean salad.

She pours oil on troubled waters.

She waters the daffodils.

She never rains.

She showers.

She buzzes her head.

She hums.

She drones.

She counts. She sorts.

She: out of sorts.

She's out on a limb.

She limps.

She wilts.

She droops.

She drips coffee on the floor.

She sips.

She slips on wet tiles.

She sinks.

## CRITERIA

1. A a actions all an and and and and and and Anxiety appointments are are are as associated be be be because been before behaviours better better biological Both can Category causes checking compulsions compulsions compulsive constitute control cope day deep depending dirty disorder disorder Disorders disruptive each Etiology everyday everyday example excessive explore extremely features feel feel for For for for found from functioning functions gaining good hands has has have he he helpful his house how how in In in in inability include individual individual individuals infected irrational irritation is is issues issues it key late learning leaving like making medication Medication more most must neutralize numerous obsessions obsessions obsessions obsessive OCD OCD OCD of of of of of often often or or or or or order otherwise perform persistent persistent point prescribed Prognosis Prognosis psychological Psychotherapy range relief responds rooted school seemingly skin stressors such Symptoms temporary that the the The the the the the the the the the these this this this thoughts thoughts thoughts thoughts throughout time times to to to to to to to to Treatment unclean uncontrollable uncontrollable underlying underlying upon used washes washing ways which which who wide with with with work would you your

## TREATMENT

2. a a A and and and and and anxiety, anxiety. anxiety—that
are are As asked asked away be be begin behaviour behaviour.
behaviours. big catastrophic Cognitive cognitive Cognitive-
behavioural components: compulsive compulsive compulsive
compulsive control disorder don't door effective exaggerated
example, Exposure exposure feel. focuses for For for from from
get go gradually hand handle hands have healthy if in In involves
involves is its learn might need obsession. obsessive obsessive
obsessive-compulsive O C D O C D of of of of of on on over own.
part perform prevented prevention public reduce refrain repeated
resorting responding response responsibility restroom rid
ritual sense sit some source teaching that the the the the the the
the Then then therapy therapy therapy this thoughts thoughts
thoughts, to to to to to to to to to touch two urge usually wash
washer, washing. way, ways will with without you you you you
you you you you you your your your your your you'd

**PROGNOSIS**

3. aaaaaaaaaaaaaaaaaaaaaaaaaaaaaaaaaaaaaaaaaaaaaaaaaaaaaaa
aaaaaAAbbbbbbbbbbbbbbbbbbbbBcccccccccccccccccccccccccccccc
ccccCCCCddddddddddddddddddddddddddddddddddddddddddddd
ddDDDDeeeeeeeeeeeeeeeeeeeeeeeeeeeeeeeeeeeeeeeeeeeeeeeeeeeee
eeeeeeeeeeeeeeeeeeeeeeeeeeeeeeeeeeeeeeeeeeeeeeeeeeeeeeeeeeee
eeeeeeeeeeeeeeeEffffffffffffffffffffFgggggggggggggggggggggggggg
gghhhhhhhhhhhhhhhhhhhhhhhhhhhhhhhhhhhhhhhhhhhhhhh
hhhhhhhhhhhiiiiiiiiiiiiiiiiiiiiiiiiiiiiiiiiiiiiiiiiiiiiiiiiiiiiiiiiiiiiiiiiiiii
iiiiiiiiiiiiiiiikkkkkkkIllllllllllllllllllllllllllllllllllllllllmmmmmmmmmm
mmmmmmmmmmmmMnnnnnnnnnnnnnnnnnnnnnnnnnnnn
nnnnnnnnnnnnnnnnnnnnnnnnnnnnnnnnnnnnnnnnnnnnnnnnnn
nnnnooooooooooooooooooooooooooooooooooooooooooooooo
ooooooooooooooooooooooooooooooooooooooooooooooooooo
ooooooooooOOOppppppppppppppppppppppppppPPPrrrrrrrrrrrrrrr
rrrrrrrrrrrrrrrrrrrrrrrrrrrrrrrrrrrrrrrrrrrrrrrrrrrssssssssssssssssssss
ssssssssssssssssssssssssssssssssssssssssssssssssssssssssssssssssssssssss
ssssStttttttttttttttttttttttttttttttttttttttttttttttttttttttttttttttttttttttt
tttttttttTTuuuuuuuuuuuuuuuuuuuuuuuuuuuuuuuuuuuuuuuuuvvv
vvvvvvvvvwwwwwwwwwwwwwwxxxxxyyyyyyyyyyyyyyyyyyyy
yyyyyz

Chip

## CHIP

She chips.

She chips her tooth on a stale raisin she pulls from the space
between the stovetop and counter next to the sink where she
knocked it yesterday stirring apple chunks, cinnamon, and
raisins into her morning oatmeal.

She chips the ice from her Grand Am's windshield.

She chips in to replace the coffee maker at the office.

She chips off the old block.

Her chips are down.

She: cheap as chips.

She hips.

She hip-checks.

She cashes in her chips.

She cheaps.

She dines and dashes.

Pays hip service.

She zips. Pants.

She hip hugs.

She jumps hip.

Her hips pass in the night.

She shapes up or hips out.

She's on everybody's hips.

Joined at the lip.

Read her hips:
She spits chips.
Buttons her lip.
He chips her shoulder.
From hip to toe
She hips the scales.
Curls her hips
Smacks her lips
She hips up a batch of cookies.
Chocolate chip.

## CRACKING

Step on a crack: break your mother's back.

Leave a dirty spoon in the sink: fail your driver's test.

Tip over a family photo:

Wash your hands for only 23 seconds: step on a crack.

Eat your green beans before your broccoli: skip a period.

Wear the blue skirt with yellow flowers: miss the last bus for
   work.

Double- not triple-check the stove is off:

migraine. Smoke three cigarettes instead of four before 5 P.M.
   Skip the bus. Don't make it to the bedroom before the front
   door closes. Lose your job. Miss your test. Break your family
   photo. Drop the rent down a sewer grate.

Forget to check your rearview mirror: run over a cat. Step on
   a family photo. Forget your hands. Check your mirror. Your
   parents split up and your sister moves across the country. Eat
   your dirty spoon. Tip over the stove. Check your mirror. Go
   to court. Double-triple-check your mirror. Wash the blue skirt
   with yellow flowers. Eat green beans before 5 P.M. Leave a dirty
   stove. Check your mirror. Double-check your hands. Lose the
   cat. Don't close the front door. Check your—

Step on a crack.

## DISHDRAINER

Bee liked to wash other people's dishes. She bit her bottom lip
    with her right canine, the one that stuck out in photos
and closed her eyes, round cheeks pressing under her eyelashes
    every time a piece
of tomato
or squash
slid between her fingers off a plate and down the drain. She
    always started with the stuck-on starches
rice, pasta, mashed potatoes, stew-burned pots, and soaked them
    in sudsy water while she tackled greasy fingerprints on wine
    glasses. She curled her toes as she glanced at the softening
    grains, detaching from the stainless steel and floating to the
    top of the grey water. Bee ran the coarse side of a yellow/green
    sponge across the pot's sticky edges, colliding with the residue.
She pushed her tongue between her front teeth, slightly, feeling
    the loose grains slide away across her hand, and float around
    the pot, shivered when the drain filled with onion skin, pieces
    of stale bread and carrot peelings, right before she reached into
    the suds and dragged
her middle finger in a circle, pushing debris through the tiny
    drain holes, breaking it up as she pressed. She tapped her
    knees together and swayed
as the water guzzled down, leaving the sink with a tide mark she

could sponge away with the yellow side, before wiping down
the water spots on the metal taps 'til the sun bounced off them.
Bee guessed what other people had eaten as she washed away the
remnants. As the water hit the pot, the garlic and rosemary
tickled the hairs in her nostrils. Bee wiped the crumbs off
a romantic dinner for two, collected them in a napkin, and
shook them into her skirt pocket.

## OCTOBER 9TH

*When you are insane, you are busy being insane—all the time...*
*When I was crazy, that was all I was.*
– Sylvia Plath

Contemplate taking a shower.

Pace living room in a diamond pattern touching two of four walls on each pass.

Sweep floors.

Mop.

Wipe up excess dust with electrostatic cloths.

Change mop head. Re-mop.

Rub out the streaks with a clean sock.

Dig a good pen and fresh notebook out of the desk drawer.

Underline the space for a title.

Start a new page. Use a ruler.

Jot a grocery list in the top-right corner: macintosh apples, garlic, cream cheese.

Cross out cream cheese.

Drink eleven glasses of water.

Open word processor.

Save blank document: "October 9th."

Unblock WebMD from internet browser.

Google malaria symptoms.

Cycle to medical laboratory. Seven kilometres.

Shake.

Chew inside lip.

Lose six vials of blood.

Scratch mosquito bites.

Bike seven point two kilometres home. Hold breath through construction dust.

Bleach kitchen counters. Rinse with warm water. Wipe down with tea tree oil. Rinse with cold water. Wipe with Lysol cloths. Dispose.

Examine bike tires for feathers.

Check for blood.

Take transit to the mall.

Purchase pregnancy test four-pack.

Cramp in right calf.

Bump into shoppers in the aisles.

Set off alarms by standing too near the entrance.

Call clinic and demand an appointment.

Vomit in a planter.

Check for blood.

Cover face with scarf.

Call back. Demand cancellations.

Search bag on the bus for stolen goods.

Read same sentence twelve times: Warranty void after six months. Warranty void after six months. Warranty void after. Warranty void after six months. Warranty void. Warranty void after six months. Warranty void after six months. Warranty void after six months. Warranty void after. Warranty after six. Warranty void after six months. Warranty void.

Open fridge.

Close.

Read same

Open cupboards.

Open warranty.

Examine shoe for feathers. Blood.

Rearrange spices by colour instead of name

> : thyme, saffron, rosemary, paprika, coriander, cinnamon, chili, black pepper, basil
>
> : saffron, paprika, chili, cinnamon, coriander, thyme, rosemary, basil, black pepper

Open fridge. Count eggs.

Check for blood.

Run out of toilet paper.

Call lab for results.

Phonebook walk-ins.

Chew inside lip.

Check for blood.

Count aspirins. 31.

Shut drawer on shirt.

Shut shirt into drawer.

Re-count aspirins. 31. 30.

Open drawer, fold shirt. Slam. Open. Shut.

Tuck passport into thigh-high boot.

Weight. 129.

Collect urine. Weight. 128.

Fold kitchen napkins.

Check for blood.

Call Telehealth. Spit feathers.

Check for blood.

Check.

Warranty.

## SELF-PORTRAIT IN STICKY NOTES

1. STOP.

before you trash that item,

EITHER:

> banana peels cores stale bread seeds cereal egg shells the
> decomposing green peppers from the crisper dead plant
> droppings on desk bathroom sink hair shavings yesterday's
> salad? Place in compost buckets on kitchen island left-hand
> side (when standing in front of water cooler). Empty buckets
> into composter (back-alley corner wall, west of garbage cans)
> when full. Wash buckets with soap and water. Hot water.
> Rinse. Dry (with blue-stripe dish towel, not red).

OR:

> cans bottles (no plastic caps!) plastic yogurt tubs margarine
> tubs (no strawberry clamshells!) cardboard toilet paper rolls
> newspaper aluminum foil pizza boxes (no grease!) phone
> bills (paid) inter-office memos (half-read) sticky notes with
> no stick left take-out menus? Place in recycling bin in back
> hallway. Red for paper products blue for plastic and cans
> (no clamshells!) Drag to front curb east of parking lot every
> second Wednesday.

For questions or concerns, consult guide to recycling and
composting under spine-shaped chiropractic office magnet on
freezer door.

2. Are **you** the person who toothpaste-spit spots the faucet in the 3rd floor women's bathroom every morning break?

3. All postings should be type-written on white paper. Do not waste full sheets of computer paper. Do not post notices on coffee pot. Do not use cursive writing. Do not use Comic Sans or Papyrus.

4. Eat me.

5. Please do not eat me.

6. The ants win when you leave leftover taco dip and dirty forks in the sink.

7. The Rapture falls tomorrow. Please remember to clean out refrigerator. Do not forget the butter dish. Post-Rapture, please use butter dish for butter products only (not leaky packets of take-out soy and plum sauce).

8. Replace: bleach Vim green peppers Lysol Wipes mop head garbage bags

9. Who dumped the pile of sugar on the floor and hid the broom?

10. Replace: sugar broom ant poison

11. If you continue to leave dirty mugs and spoons on the counter next to the sink: your cat will catch flu and vomit in your bed, your Fiesta will lose a side mirror in the night, you will drop your wallet down a sewer grate and trip over the bottom of your pants, skin your knees, frighten a skunk, and be late for a promotion interview (for which you will forget your updated resumé). You will also lose your electric stapler privileges for three weeks.

12. If you need to bring cough syrup to the office, you are audibly hacking and expelling mucus. Go home and keep your germs to yourself. Please.

## OXFORD CLASSICS DICTIONARY

Jay updates me: news in dishwashing, 90s television series(es)?
    what books are you teaching and how many dates have you
    had since the beginning of September? Remember when I said
    I'd talk to your therapist?—How many years has—How many
    tomatoes have we—How many episodes of *Buffy*—
Where did you end up living? Is cleaning better on your own with
    your own lamps, tablecloths, coffee pots, hallway mirror—
    What does your school call it, a homecoming? Why does the
    football team yell about it on the bus in the—coming home to
    the kitchen to the cauliflower and spinach for a pot of soup—
    from itch from claw—to a birthday cake light on the icing
    (lopsided)
What's the diagnosis today, Jay?
for me: dishwashing, draining, drying, alphabetizing, polishing
    wood, and sanitizing sports equipment.
For Jay: today she's imposter syndrome (there's a lot of lit on the
    topic, she says)
and last time what were the symptoms last time?
blood clots, leaks, or shaky limbs.
At her place, there's too much politics. Nobody in her apartment's
    indoors on a Saturday night.
We can both agree about Leonard Cohen
but tonight she isn't sure.

That imposter syndrome sneaks up.

She gets lost in outside fields unless they're wheat, or poppies, or
uncut grass—fields that leave organic matter on her shoes and
the knees of her tights (not political theory or classics)

I thought for years classics meant the Oxford kind, or at a push
Penguin—a new edition of Brontë or Dickinson, with the same
16pt Garamond font on the cover, a black box, some white
lines, and a brooding inset from a watercolour painting of a
castle. I re-bought a whole set, 13 books I already owned so
they could match (now that's good marketing). Jay underlines
the acronym for the *Oxford Classics Dictionary.*

## PRIMETIME SOAP

Peter and Lee-Ann are fighting in the bookie's again. During
the commercial for Palmolive I've got time to wash four plates
before we find out what happened to Gail's new husband. New
sponge warm water new suds rice sliding down plates into the
strainer I can't cut the grease the spots on these glasses so it's
back in the sink water getting cold so refill and more soap from
the Costco dispenser on sale half the price of buying it at Metro.
Back on, I hear Manchester accents arguing about the underwear
company and who's going to get a round in at the local. These
glasses still filthy orange pulp sticking to the bottom rim and oily
fingermarks from an Ontario June. Must be a wedding because
there's bells and someone storming in the back of the church but
the soap's all gone, water's grey, re-fill the sink more squirts of
green liquid. I'll get back to the couch before more adverts about
hockey night later and some *Canadian Idol* CD. But this grease
really won't rub off and how dirty is that dishdrainer the wipes
will kill 99.9 percent of bacteria but they burn my fingertips
wrinkly and pink back in the water to wash off the disinfectant.
Theme tune is on again and that cat meow that starts every
episode maybe a repeat of the one before I can catch the bits
where I was washing. These damn dishes soy sauce might be the
pattern on the plate, an imperfection in the paint unless I just
need a new sponge and some more soap. The wedding's already

over? Liam's back from the honeymoon and chatting in the pub? Cold water around the sink and my hands shake a bit. Sort out their wrinkles so I can get back to the couch. Just as soon as. The grease off these dishes.

## COMPOST BIN

Rot leaking from a crack in the old yogurt tub on the kitchen
    counter and dripping onto the tile floor because:
        you were late for work
        you grabbed a granola bar and ran for the bus
        your nose was stuffy. you didn't smell the mould.

I scooped up the cores egg celery avocado coffee plum banana
    mash in a plastic dollar-store bag and dangled the wet mess
    between two fingers drip drip coffee and rot on the rug

Your bed:
        sheets in a ball at the footboard
        blanket on the carpet under two T-shirts and a
        pair of dirty boxers
        plate and fork stuck to hard penne noodles
        toenail clippings
        a green clementine orange between the head
        board and mattress
        damp and chunky with rotting tomato and
        banana leak

The compost in your bed:

> three apple cores
> four egg shells with yolks
> the ends off one stick of celery
> one four-week-old avocado
> a recycled paper filter full of no-name brand
> coffee grinds
> the pits of three plums
> one banana skin, yellow, and one brown banana

I dragged my hand through the shells / broke open the avocado
   skin / smeared green and brown gel and taupe across your
   pillowcase

You're out of Vim.
I sanitized the old yogurt tub compost and taped the crack up
   with a piece of masking tape I dug out of your junk drawer
lined the tub with a plastic drugstore bag and threw away your
   receipt for Nyquil and chocolate
bleached the countertops, rinsed the sink, made the bed, pushed
   shirts and boxers under the rug, kicked your sweaty towels
   down the stairs

I scrubbed my hands
ate a plum from the crisper
swallowed the pit.

Peel

## PEEL

She peels.

She peels a potato.

She peels an apple and eats only the skin.

She peels the 50-percent-off sticker from the underside of her
  black patent leather pump.

She peels burnt skin off the backs of her calves.

She flakes. She sheds. She gardens. She tools.

She shacks up with her ex.

She peels the sheets off her bed.

She peels the polish off her nails. In sheets.

He peels the tights from her thighs.

She appeals her parking ticket.

She peels a grape.

She scrapes. She rinds.

She grates a lemon for zest.

She grates on my nerves.

She peels down the wrong side of the road.

She peels away the skin at the sides of her thumbs.

She peels off her wet dress.

She strips the colour from her hair.

She trips and skins her palms on the sidewalk.

Sheet rips.

She stains.

Sheet use.

She chews.

She chews her bottom lip.

She peels her eyes.

She keeps them peeled.

## 1C WESTBOUND 12:45 A.M.

she's mouthing
her finger toothing the skinflap down the side of one nail

           teeth on

           teeth

           CLICK

           CLICK

           CLICK

           CLICK

           CLICK


           CLICK

runs a raw index fingernail
down the side of her thumb
bites
tooth on tooth           CLICK

thin fingers raw red
rips in corners like plum jam edges
hands like rows of crêpes

tooth tooth and nail

           CLICK

    shards teeth tearing into raw red corners

fingertips wrinkle from spit
and 57 years

                                        CLICK


                                        CLICK


thumbing her incisor
incising fingertips
she brushes blue bead glasses chain back
behind her ears
ears and cheeks and glasses un-
bit
bite-free
toothless
jam stain fingers
                                        CLICK
                                        CLICK


pulls the yellow stop cable
wrinkle wet fingertips leave
damp prints on windowglass

freeze

CLICK

brakes hiss

CLICK

## LARYNGITIS

Em's a hummer. Lost her voice at the wrestling match talking
lingerie over the announcer. A strapless bra. A sentence thaw?
Skipped Tuesday night karaoke to seal the cracks in her throat.
Couldn't fingerspell fast enough. Hopped a cab to track down
her chords at the Friday night ska show. Waited four hours in
the ER scratching her hummingbird necklace two syllables
emmmm emm at the triage counter. Ear / nose / throat. Musta
slipped up and out your sinus cavity. Remember when you used
to laugh pop out your nose? Same general concept. Replacement
parts aren't available any closer than Woodstock but FedEx has
overnight service if you're willing to pay. Emmmmm...mmm
mmm in the negative. Em patches up her throat with pieces of an
old softball. Mmmmms and emms along to Doo Doo Doo on the
radio. Cuts and pastes. Sews. Swallows. Croaks down the hallway.
Ems and ahs. Hums if you kiss her. Em's a hummer.

## STREET LEVEL

Montréal you bruise me. Laptop bag tote umbrella scarf gloves
leg muscle bones push through damp crowds into un-turning
turnstile bars. Red light. *Carte expiré. Re-essayez s.v.p.* 9:30
squinting through hail for wine at 210 Fairmount Ouest slip
past the glass doors half litre waiting at 201. Tarmac melting
with four feet of snow right boot plumbs a sidewalk river: two
centimetres above my knee and rising fast through tights like
food colouring climbs a celery stalk. Eaton Centre says: one
hundred forty dollars for red rubber boots but sorry! Sold out.
New shipment Wednesday morning. McGill métro *en direction
d'Angrignon, the one with the A, not the H. Honoré. Quelque chose
comme ça.* Headphones shuffling down Laurier leak upstairs:
Chelsea Hotel #2. *Connaissez-vous la rue Rachel? Est-ce que c'est
en ce direction?* Toes wrinkling in wet socks straddle puddles
on Saint Denis choose road-edge ice skating over sidewalk
swimming until hipbone cracks asphalt rink skirt bleeds blue dye
into smarting thigh. Fifty-two steps down, limping, *Mademoiselle,
il y a un ascenseur!* up to street level Saint Laurent staircase pull at
bruise edges spreading *souvenirs gratuits.*

## SELF-PORTRAIT WITH BRUISES

*Some women marry houses.*
*It's another kind of skin*
 – "Housewife," Anne Sexton


Some women marry roller skates
Soles fuse to plates and wheels
slip of the tailbone
scrape wrist
trip toe.
Laces taut
wrap bearings
tug grooves in ankles.
She rubs cream onto green purple knees shaving around stubble
    swell
pulls tights over thigh blotches
wheel-round fleshy.
Legs that bruise like plums.

## STEALING FROM THE EMERGENCY ROOM

Keep your head on straight
or tilt to the left. Focus
on a stable wall
read the sign: EMBER ASH OR
ANDS
Above the fountain
outside the bathroom. Get inside
the words
RE: SOR S
just keep
still even if your eyes don't
focus
break signs into words
R / ASH OUR AD
into letters
R E M   H D
just don't let yourself
un-tilt
His and
HAND
AN/IN/IS
YOU/OR
you too help—

start again

how in any

inside this

AN/ IN IS DER

AM /AN PRE/THE PRE/ OF

a prevention of

AN/IN fection

an inability to prevent

PRE/FECTION

re-WASH YOUR

ANDS


AN/I

YOU/R

not preventing

/RE

IN FECTION

REM/ EMBER

ASH

your ANDS

PRE/ MEMBER

VENT RE

WAS

IN / OUR

ANDS

## BIKE LANE

Write on my leg in oil from the underside of your car

or

Write on my leg with the underside of your car

or

I'm not

but there's oil on my leg

and blood on your bumper

a shock of fabric from my Made in Bangladesh designer knock-
off summer dress,

the one with the polka dots and the Peter Pan collar

There's oil on the collar that used to be white

but the oil on my leg might be from my bicycle chain

my bicycle under your car and there's some blue paint on your
bumper

and scratches on my bicycle so you can see the primer

so you can see you smoked me

took me out so hard my bell got crushed

before I could ring it

red ribbon from my basket gutter wet

You sped up like I was a squirrel who'd somehow get out of the
way

You'd've stopped for a skunk

Next time I'll wear stripes instead of spots

But for now I wear raw stripes up my ankle

clipped my pedal and pulled me under

two boxes of Weetabix and a carton of unsweetened soy leaking

    down an asphalt crack

Crushed so I've got nothing for dinner

I'm under your car writing in blood

or is it oil on my leg?

My sandal flung across the street;

pink and red in the road

the hot grey undercarriage of your car maybe a pickup

where I can write on my leg or the metal

between the tarmac and your undercarriage

or is it oil?

## BLACK FRIDAY

Propofol feels like Drano smells like silicone tubing tastes like
rice crackers sounds like post-nasal drip looks like a moustache
feels like nylon stitches smells like dust tastes like Tylenol 3
sounds like a tissue box looks like a drip of snot hovering at the
end of your nose feels like cotton wool smells like a Q-tip tastes
like ice chips sounds like a humidifier looks like wool socks feels
like a clogged drain smells like a remote control tastes like a
blood clot sounds like a thick blanket looks like McDonald's soft
serve feels like a period smells like an advent calendar tastes like a
notebook sounds like an i.v. feels like a popsicle stick smells like
a car seat tastes like gauze sounds like water boiling looks like an
itch feels like a re-run smells like a gag reflex tastes like a tissue
sounds like flowers looks like a sink plug feels like a trunk tastes
like mild manners sounds like a lucky penny looks like a whistle
feels like cauliflower smells like the carpet tastes like napkins
sounds like a cart with a wonky wheel looks like a Christmas ball
feels like Black Friday.

→ gross things you don't want
→ chaotic enery (black friday

## SELF-PORTRAIT ON ASPHALT

Split skin
dragged a trail of elbow along the sidewalk
skipstones and beerglass nesting deep
bloodslip slick wrist /
mosquito lumps / cut cuticles /
sneakers scuff armhair /
black cotton shirt sleeve scraps /
sunburned flesh
off pavement
bikes tread tissue and sweat
with gum grit and saliva
sun baking forearm to asphalt
gravel fuses to bone
peel heatseals
sears limb to path
tarmac garnish
sidewalk scab

## SLUSH

Slushing through the side of the road

jujubes, Scattergories, and hefting canvas bags of public library
mysteries

no inscriptions in first editions under glass in my study

no study

the girl who knits backwards, never learned to swim, can't lace a
figure skate

"buy me a bowl of mushroom soup at the café on the corner, a
tap dance lesson, a brown roll, an ant farm, a bus ticket with a
transfer to the 1A"

words stack up in my throat, backed-up serifs scratching their
way through like nacho chips

I wrap three red scarves one over the other over the other around
my neck and chin and lips and forehead

fingers damp with saliva

backs in knots. door in doors

pushes open without a key; you never remember to slam it on
your way out

before I make it to the hallway closet, dump my soggy coat and
slog off boots

you know I can't stand to hear about any mat I can't trample in
the hall

my eyes squint from smears on the kitchen window

to the mop and bucket, cold water
I'll be bald soon if I'm counting the strands of hair on the tiles
and bone if you collect the dry flakes
sinuses and teeth skinning remnants on a Swiffer cloth
my underwear on the floor under the table
more klicks away than I can count on my fingers

## SLICK

My legs sweat and prickle
I hold onto your wrist to keep from slipping off the bed.
The landlord dropped off an air conditioner but I can't turn down
   the noise.
In the fridge, floating on dirty summer melt
Tupperware containers full of lentil soup I'll never swallow.
The sodden rug over the radiator steams
waits for winter when it can freeze and stiffen.
Over my head I smell the cracks in the upstairs floorboards
worms in April gutters, compost bucket coffee grinds
plaster wet and dropping in chunks off the ceiling.
We drip
half-waiting for a tidal wave to burst through the vents.

## RECIPE

Last night an abscess:
       red and furious
       seeping through the top of my sock
damp grey cotton clinging
to taut skin.
In the kitchen, I pour
boiling water over a fork
expose and puncture
dig prongs deep into the raw mound
and the smell!
Not like the cat's
sore when it burst: sour cheese, acrid and retching
but:
spicy jalapeño,
coriander, garlic.
I press with both thumbs.
my foot issues:
       a kidney bean
       clumps of ground beef
       tomato juice
hot chili drips between my toes
bits of onion slide over tendons
slip into the carpet as I hop

holding the leaky foot level
hop
to the cupboard for a plate
and the fridge for a slice of bread
to sop up my mess.

## STEMS

1.

I've got the best legs in poetry.
The audience at the open mic took a vote
my calves most worthy of macramé leggings and a miniskirt
from our generous local sponsor,
the girl with the hook, third row from the stage
send her stats after the show
thigh circumference with a shoelace and a metre stick
subtract a few centimetres
(for good measure)

2.

Cowboy hat at the karaoke bar thinks I've got
*Nice stems (baby)*
green and waxy
feet like cut flowers
thorny and brown
*A guy can't tell a girl he likes her legs? Maybe you should wear a*
  *longer skirt.*
Cover up my stems?
heels sink into mud
root me to the ground
cowboy tips his hat I turn

on one wedge, a thorn

in his boot


3.

On primetime, "having" legs, arms, ears, fingernails means

having limbs

in a jar

a meat locker

in a plastic garbage bag at the bottom of the lake

I've got the smoothest legs, the right one in a bag of wool, top
    shelf of the closet

waiting for winter

the left behind the wok in the pots and pans drawer

the pinkest ears chill in the fridge

the thinnest wrists in my typewriter case

the thickest toenails between the pages of an old *Spin* magazine

the softest soles strung on the backyard washing line

two lips in the garden compost

a pinky finger on top of the microwave

and one eyebrow caught under the back-door shoe rack.

## THE FLOOD

We lost 14 pounds of blueberries in the flood. Freezer-seal
cracked waves lifting tidy date-labelled Ziploc bags August 26th
29th September 12th through the laundry room and up the
stairs, out the back door, into the creek downstream and then
the St. Clair River. Blue bubbles dry stems bobbed in moss water,
tempting fish like lures where the hook never follows. The next
night it rained again, storm-of-a-century the early morning
newscaster dripped wool pants leaching up to the knees. The
river gluts the street, pours down sewers, rushes up through
drains in every laundry room and cellar in the city, tipping bottles
of bleach, wine, beer, and fabric softener. Neighbours sop, heap
carpet scraps, and split chipboard furniture roadside wet-vaccing
up wads of toilet paper, hands over nose and mouth. Gag. Bail.
Trashed sodden shoes. Algae socks. Toe wrinkle. Raining feces,
silt, blueberries. 1B pulped two rolls of 60s vintage wrapping
paper. Thirsty paisley. Cardboard buckled. Lost a bucket of
sidewalk chalk, red recycling bin down the road. Lost a box
of pancake mix, headlines from last year's newspapers, plastic
raincoat, bicycle pump. Found stray leaky letters clinging to
baseboards SOR FI EN HE. Found a pile of blueberries softening
under the rug.

## INSERT BODY TEXT

this poem has legs
smooth shoulders warm thigh
jeans fall off the bone
dry heels flaking skin under one eye
two pimples on the neck, buried
pigeon toes
a broken rib can't hide under breast fat
knee bruises hip bruises shoulder
bruises dandruff acne scars burn marks knee scars shoulder scars
    elbow
scars skin splitting between fingers elbows bleeding
nape tight calves
stubble
should I mention ass lips tongue eyes dimples toes
and what if by the end of all this you want to fuck?
Or never touch pen to paper again?
Can a poem turn a trick?
Is this page too transparent? panty lines, breath lines
Does the corner slip down, uncover the lace edge
of a notebook?
pen scratching neck
bite a lip / tongue / tooth
but how do you read indents?

Curl toes in a watermark
did you print them or did I?
my body of work | pressing warm sheets into your hands

## ACKNOWLEDGEMENTS

Without the feedback of the following people, this book would not exist: Many thanks to Nicole Markotić (who tolerated lots of bad puns but very few clichés), Alex Gayowsky, Jordan Turner, Braydon Beaulieu, Jasmine Elliott, and Josh Kolm (for always contributing an edit or thirty). I'm also extremely grateful to Jay and Hazel MillAr and their staff at BookThug for taking a chance on my poems and for this beautiful book.

I am indebted to my family and friends for their endless patience and support: Len, Jill, and Stephen Hargreaves, Vajo Stajic, and the Border City Brawlers roller derby league (for much encouragement, and the latter for many bruises as well).

This project was supported by grants from the Social Sciences and Humanities Research Council of Canada (SSHRC), the Ontario Graduate Scholarship (OGS), and the University of Windsor.

Versions of poems from *Leak* have appeared in the following publications: *Cuizine, Descant, The Feathertale, Canada and Beyond, The Windsor Review, Whisky Sour City* and *Detours*. Italicized portions of "Paper Ladder" are borrowed from "Michi's Ladder, " an eating plan created by the Beach Body Company.

KATE HARGREAVES is a writer and roller derby skater. Her first book, *Talking Derby: Stories from a Life on Eight Wheels* (2012), is a collection of short prose vignettes inspired by women's flat-track roller derby. Her poetry has been published in literary journals across North America, including *Descant, filling Station, The Puritan, Drunken Boat, The Antigonish Review, Canada and Beyond, Carousel*, and *Rampike*, in the anthologies *Whisky Sour City* (2012), *Detours* (2012), as well as in the *Windsor Review's* "Best Writers Under 35" issue. Hargreaves was the recipient of a Windsor Endowment for the Arts Emerging Literary Artist Award in 2011 and a Governor General's Gold Medal in Graduate Studies at the University of Windsor in 2012, where she obtained her Bachelor's and Master's degrees in English & Creative Writing. Kate grew up in Amherstburg, Ontario, but now lives in Windsor, where she works as a publishing assistant and book designer.

## COLOPHON

First Edition, fall 2014.

Distributed in Canada by the Literary Press Group: www.lpg.ca

Distributed in the USA by Small Press Distribution: www.spdbooks.org

Shop online at www.bookthug.ca

Copy edited by Ruth Zuchter

Type + design by Jay MillAr